Amber's New Family

Amber's New Family

Elizabeth Cameron

Amber's New Family

This book is written to provide information and motivation to readers. Its purpose is not to render any type of psychological, legal, or professional advice of any kind. The content is the sole opinion and expression of the author, and not necessarily that of the publisher.

Copyright © 2021 by Elizabeth Cameron.

All rights reserved. No part of this book may be reproduced, transmitted, or distributed in any form by any means, including, but not limited to, recording, photocopying, or taking screenshots of parts of the book, without prior written permission from the author or the publisher. Brief quotations for noncommercial purposes, such as book reviews, permitted by Fair Use of the U.S. Copyright Law, are allowed without written permissions, as long as such quotations do not cause damage to the book's commercial value. For permissions, write to the publisher, whose address is stated below.

Printed in the United States of America.

ISBN 978-1-955363-02-0 (Paperback)
ISBN 978-1-955363-03-7 (Digital)

Lettra Press books may be ordered through booksellers or by contacting:

Lettra Press LLC
30 N Gould St. Suite 4753
Sheridan, WY 82801
1 307-200-3414 | info@lettrapress.com
www.lettrapress.com

To my children you're my inspiration and joy. It's a journey I would never want to miss: our joys and sorrows, our achievements and failures and most of all the love our family share together and knowing how important you are to me forever and always.

Introduction

Parenthood has many surprises. It doesn't come with instructions, but the journey is full of joy, tears and challenges filled with lots of love and adventures. To parents new and experienced love, the journey, share the love, embrace life to the fullest. We laugh, we learn, we make mistakes but in the end love and family are the most important thing we can pass on to our children and grandchildren.

Amber and Midnight had a long courtship and soon decided to become partners for life. They got married in the village by the mayor . It was a grand affair celebrating late into the night .They loved each other and took care of each other and soon they found a comfortable cave and made it their home happily being together and enjoying life together.

Once life settled down for George, Amber and Midnight set about getting their cave home comfortable for the coming winter. George would visit and spend time with them. Soon life settles into a comfortable routine for amber and midnight they would fly at sunset watching the moon rise and the stars twinkle in the velvet sky. And sometimes take George with them on small trips like they used to. Their friendship had deepened over time and it was very strong.

But soon Amber started feeling different and felt more tired. Midnight was worried about her and so was George but when she started digging a nest George figured out amber was heavy with eggs and soon, she would be laying her eggs. Amber lined her nest with straw and soft furs and one fine spring day Amber laid 3 beautiful golden eggs.

George was so proud of Amber; Midnight was shocked and awed by what Amber had done and as she rested Midnight nuzzled her and she fell asleep the thought that he was going to be a dad hit him. He felt scared and happy at the same time worried would he be a good dad. Amber reassured him as he laid down beside her that he would be a great dad and he would be a great protector as well and gentle and loving too and she nuzzled him and they both fell asleep filled with love and wonder of the day.

George helped Amber and Midnight care for the eggs and after a few months the eggs started to rock violently and crack as the dragonettes burst from their eggs George came and was there when the little dragons hatched out of their eggs.

George remembered the day Amber hatched how small and fragile she was and so beautiful. Midnight was overwhelmed by the feeling of love that enveloped him as he looked at his babies as Amber cleaned the babies and curled around them to warm them Midnight looked on with pride of his family.

Midnight hunted for the babies first meal and watched as they ate with gusto, they were asking for more and he gave it to them when they were full, they curled up and fell asleep, happy and full they dreamed happy dreams. George hugged the new babies and greeted them with a gentle kiss welcoming them to the world and all its wonders.

George hugged Amber and told her how much he loved her and how proud he was of her and Midnight and their precious babies.

Amber and Midnight set about their new responsibilities as parents learning to care for their brood sometimes making mistakes and learning from them and feeling pride as the babies grew and learned how to walk, learning to use their wings though they were clumsy and uncoordinated they had the support of George and their loving parents.

They learned with loving patience and laughter, tears when they fell or hurt themselves hugs from mom and dad encouraging them to keep trying and never give up and it's OK to be sad if you don't succeed the first time you try and try again you pick yourself up and keep trying till you are successful and knowing you have done your best.

Their successes came in stages and when they made the goal, they were going for everyone celebrated and encouraged them to aim higher.

George read to them often and they would draw and color and they loved walking in the woods smelling the fresh grass and feeling the breezes on their scales tasting many things that they came across.

They watched fish swimming in a stream Bella crouched low and stalked the fish and with a wiggle she pounced it in the water. Splash into the cold water she went up to her nose the fish swam under her belly tickling her.

Midnight picked her up from the water hugging her and putting her in the grass. Bella was fearless; nothing seemed to scare her. She was the bravest of the three dragons, always looking to explore and search for interesting things and stuff. Bella loved her father's strong arms and hugs. She watched him closely when he was flying with their mother every wing beat and posture, she noted everything learning every move she wanted to fly!

Her brother Nermal was a loving soul he loved cuddling with Amber and being read to and Spending time with George daydreaming about new places seeing with wonder all that was good napping in the sun. Stalking insects and frogs watching the mice play around them.

When it came to taking naps, the youngest dragon refused to and she never wanted to miss anything she was so curious about everything there was nothing too small to explore but she was very shy and hid when things got intense her name was Rosa, she was sweet tempered and helpful.

At 6 months old Midnight and Amber took them to a secluded area and started to teach them to fly strengthening their wings and encouraging them to attempt to lift off the ground they flapped and flapped but could not do it they got frustrated and started to cry. Midnight and Amber hugged them and reassured them that it was OK and that they will get it.

It took several months for them to get strong enough to lift off the ground and once they did, they were so excited and kept wanting to do more but their parents knew that they needed to take it slow.

Every day they practiced and finally learned to fly though they could not fly far they were getting stronger every day they would take George out on short flights every day, George remembered his time with Amber as she learned to fly and watching the dragons grow made his heart fill with pride.

George wished he could show them the island where he and Amber first went to and see their first sunset on the ocean and swim in the ocean for the first time.

The dragons first birthday was rapidly approaching and George, Amber and Midnight got together to plan their first birthday as they started to plan the babies tried to sneak into the room and listen but Normal was a little clumsy and knocked the broom down so George, Amber and Midnight each took a baby and cuddled them and soon put them to bed.

They soon had it figured out what they were doing and everyone was invited. George's mother wanted to make the cakes for them feeling blessed that George had found such a good friend and the blessing the baby dragons were to all. George's father was making them special toys and his sisters were making them soft toys to cuddle.

They took turns hunting and caring for the young dragons, they never lacked for attention, someone was always there for them. There was always someone willing to give hugs and play with or read to them. After the babies were asleep George, Amber and Midnight sat by the fireplace deciding what to do and who to invite.

Of course, Cody and Robert would come Ashlie and her family would come and Samantha would come as well. Even the emperor of China came too.

With everyone working together all the preparations completed the day finally came Amber and Midnight brought out their young dragonettes to meet their friends and family on their birthday

, Rosa and Bella were led to the village square where the villagers had worked together to decorate and cook the food and prepare for guests that were arriving.

Midnight and amber flew in Samantha and her family and dropped them off then picked up Cody and Robert and then Ashlie and her family, and finally the emperor of china and his family it was a very long trip for everyone but once everyone was assembled the dragonettes were surrounded by all who loved them.

Hugs and introductions were made and the celebrations began, games were played, food was plentiful and everyone had a good time.

When the cake came out it was a sight to behold many loving hands worked on it and decorated it took many strong hands to place it in front of the dragnets their eyes filled with wonder at the huge cake Nermal took a huge bite before anyone could stop him with cake and frosting all over his face everyone laughed and then sang happy birthday to them.

They were given many gifts that day but the best gift of all was the fellowship of family and friends sharing and being together on their birthday. The celebrations went late into the night the dragonettes were put to bed and were watched by George's mother Jo Ann, she washed them up and read them a story and tucked them in. Soon they were dreaming of their birthday with smiles on their faces.

In the village people were getting to know each other, meeting family members talking about how things have been going, catching up on everything. Ashlie, Samantha, Cody and Robert sat by the fire and talked late and caught up with each other's lives and each other surprised by the many changes they have had in their lives and thrilled that Amber and Midnight had such beautiful babies and were honored that they were allowed to share this important day with them.

George, Amber, Midnight went to see the emperor and his family. They sat in a silken tent with them talking and sharing their experiences together and how big their children have grown over the time they were last together and how they have changed.

Life was going well for all and it was so nice to spend this time together after so long apart they missed the time they spent in china and the beautiful countryside there. As they sat the crickets and fireflies came out and the night sounds filled the air.

Eventually George and Amber and Midnight returned to their homes that night filled with joy and happiness to have spent time with their friends. They checked on the babies who were dreaming sweet dreams curled together in their nest all was right with the world Amber and Midnight joined their babies and slept peacefully the rest of the night.

Morning found the babies climbing all over their parents wanting to eat and play Amber and Midnight stretched and yawned and soon had them fed and ready to play they met in the square and spent the day with their friends and family in joyful celebration of life and friendship for all. After a week of celebrations everyone needed to return home and Amber and Midnight took them home promising that when the babies were strong enough, they would visit them.

After the guests had left life settled into a normal routine the babies grew stronger and learned to fly very well and soon it was time to take their first long trip as a family. George and Amber and Midnight took off at dawn as the sun was rising on the horizon the pinks and golden rays radiated setting the sky alight as the stars faded away the dragons and George flew away towards the first island, they ever visited prepared to stop and let the dragonettes rest as needed.

They stopped by the cabin George and Amber had made together. And spent a wonderful winter together. They caught Cody and Robert as they were returning from a research project ready to relax and take care of paperwork for the next project later on. They were happy to see the family and George there, everyone relaxed and food was prepared. The babies were hungry and ate well while everyone sat and ate at a more leisurely pace watching the babies play and romp.

The dragonettes fell asleep under watchful eyes and loving gazes they were very loved. Bella, Normal, and Rosa explored the woods and streams around the cabin took hikes with their parents and Cody during the rest stop being shown all the wonders of the area and playing most of the time. They went swimming in the streams and met the otters and watched them play with the fish. They watched the deer and other animals play and interact together and enjoyed short flights with their parents and their friends.

But the time came to move on goodbyes were said and hugs exchanged and off the family flew off to the ocean where they spent their first time on the island. George loved the smells and sounds of the ocean and how the waves lapped at the shore, the cries of the sea birds and watching the fish and whales swimming with their calves. Pods of dolphins playing in the surf.

They showed the dragonettes the ships sailing on the waves as dolphins raced on their bow and woke small fishing boats hauling up fish in their nets and watched the seabirds dive into the ocean catching small fish and flying away with their catch to feed their young.

They made it to the island about noon and let the dragonettes swim in the surf as Amber and Midnight caught fish George watched over them as they played and sunned themselves. Dinner was cooked over the fire and the dragonettes ate many fish that night happy and full. They cuddled the babies and read them a story and they fell asleep feeling safe and protected. They curled up and fell asleep as the moon slowly rose on the horizon safe with George and their parents dreaming of their adventures.

Amber and Midnight flew in the velvet sky as their children slept under Georges watchful eyes enjoying each other's company alone and free to be with each other to strengthen their bonds with each other. They came back and they talked into the night about plans and where they might want to go next. Then sat around the fire and relaxed enjoying each other's company watching the stars in the night sky.

Morning broke to find the dragonettes playing in the sunrise surf chasing fish and splashing in the water as George went about making breakfast for everyone once the smell of food wafted across their noses all thoughts of play went out the window and they were sitting around George waiting for the food to be ready. They ate and then they prepared to leave for the next leg of their adventures the dragonettes were excited and ready to go as final preparations were made to leave.

So off they flew the family together across the ocean watching the pods of dolphins searching for fish the water was so blue and life was abundant and interesting the dragnets enjoyed being with them and seeing everything. They made landfall at noon and made lunch and let the dragonettes rest and play.

There were large oak trees growing with lush green grass and a stream running through the area reminding George and amber of their first time adventuring together learning and building together spending the long winter exploring and enjoying the time there they thought about it but decided to move on after the dragonettes had rested enough to fly on.

They flew over valleys and fields and a few mountains as well and the sun was starting to set and it was time to set down and find a place to rest, there was a small village not too far so they went a bit more away from it warning the dragonettes to stay close. George set about cooking and sleeping places. Amber caught a deer and found some wild vegetables and grains and cooked them up. Everyone ate well and were soon resting and telling stories and listening to what everyone had to say. The dragonettes played and cuddled with their parents and George settled down for the night as the sun set.

That night everyone watched as the stars came out and twinkled brightly in the night sky and they saw a falling star streak across the sky over their heads they made wishes as it fell.

Safe from being discovered everyone fell asleep and dreamed happy dreams morning found them waking to a small kitten checking them out pouncing on their tails sniffing their noses and checking everything they had around them she was small and playful, she had calico and tabby markings a beautiful cat to see and had a very loud purr too.

The dragnets played with the kitten while breakfast was prepared for them and they shared their food with her. It was a lazy day and they went exploring the area and checking out the village they had spotted last night.

The kitten stayed in the camp when they went exploring. They saw women weaving cloth and men shearing sheep and saw children playing and doing their chores unaware they were being watched. The people seemed relaxed and happy the children played and helped their parents. Amber and Midnight showed Nermal, Rosa and Bella how to watch and not be seen.

They crept away unnoticed by the villagers and flew to the small lake they had seen and drank some water and explored the area carefully to not be seen by the villagers in the area.

They flew back to camp to find the kitten playing in the supplies she had spread everything all over and had eaten some of the food that had been packed away. She did her best to look innocent but the evidence was all around her covered in flour and something sticky all she could do was meow and purr.

Amber, George and Midnight sighed and set about cleaning up and the kitten got a bath looking like a drowned rat dripping wet. George dried her off and put her in the middle of the dragonettes as they napped, she snuggled in and slept with them.

They went through their supplies and found they needed to replace many items so George would have to go barter for what they needed. George packed up what he needed armed with a list off he hiked to the village to trade with them.

When George walked up the road leading to the village the children gathered around him curious about him and where he came from but George just smiled and entered the market to trade, a small child was petting his fur and looked up at him shyly with a smile said his fur was soft can I hug you? She was about 4 years old and was clutching a teddy bear. George asked where her mommy was and she tugged on George to follow her.

Her mother was cooking and tending the fire and had told her to stay in the yard her husband was off hunting and she had her hands full. She saw her daughter bringing George up the walk and apologized for her child being so bold. George said it was fine and asked her if it was okay if he hugged her daughter and told her daughter had asked him that is why she bought him there. Her mother said it was okay and the little girl hugged him and told her mom can I keep the big teddy bear please? George had to laugh and gently put her down.

He said no and then explained he was in need of supplies and was looking for a good trade for goods he needed she told him the best place to go and offered to trade with him if he wanted to so with his list out, he made a few trades with her and gave her daughter a carved wooden cat he had made to play with. Thinking of the kitten at the camp much as they would love to keep her, they could not and she deserved a loving home.

As he said goodbye, he quickly made his way to the market and got what he needed and a pink ribbon as well, when he made it back to camp, he told everyone of the little girl and her family. They agreed that the kitten needed a home and the little girl needed a friend so Amber and George put the pink ribbon on the kitten and flew away. They landed and Amber hid as George knocked on their door.

The mother answered the door and George told her of the kitten and that she needed a loving home and that he could not have her with him. He introduced her to the kitten and asked her if her daughter could have her? The kitten purred loudly and licked the woman's hand they had been looking for a kitten but all the ones they had seen were too wild.

She called her daughter to come to the door when she came to the door she again asked if she could keep George, again he said no but she could have the kitten in his paws instead as a gift she hugged the kitten and thanked him and ran to her bed and kissed the kitten and told her she loved her so much. The mother thanked him and would never forget him and the special gift to her daughter. The kitten was named Hestia by the little girl

George said goodbye and wished them a good day and many happy days and walked down the path heading for the gate as he opened the gate the little girl came running after him and threw herself at him giving him a hug and a kiss thanking him for the kitten, she was going to love her forever George kissed her and hugged her and told her he was glad she loved the kitten and set her down and she ran back to her house. George felt good that she was happy and knew the kitten would be loved forever and always.

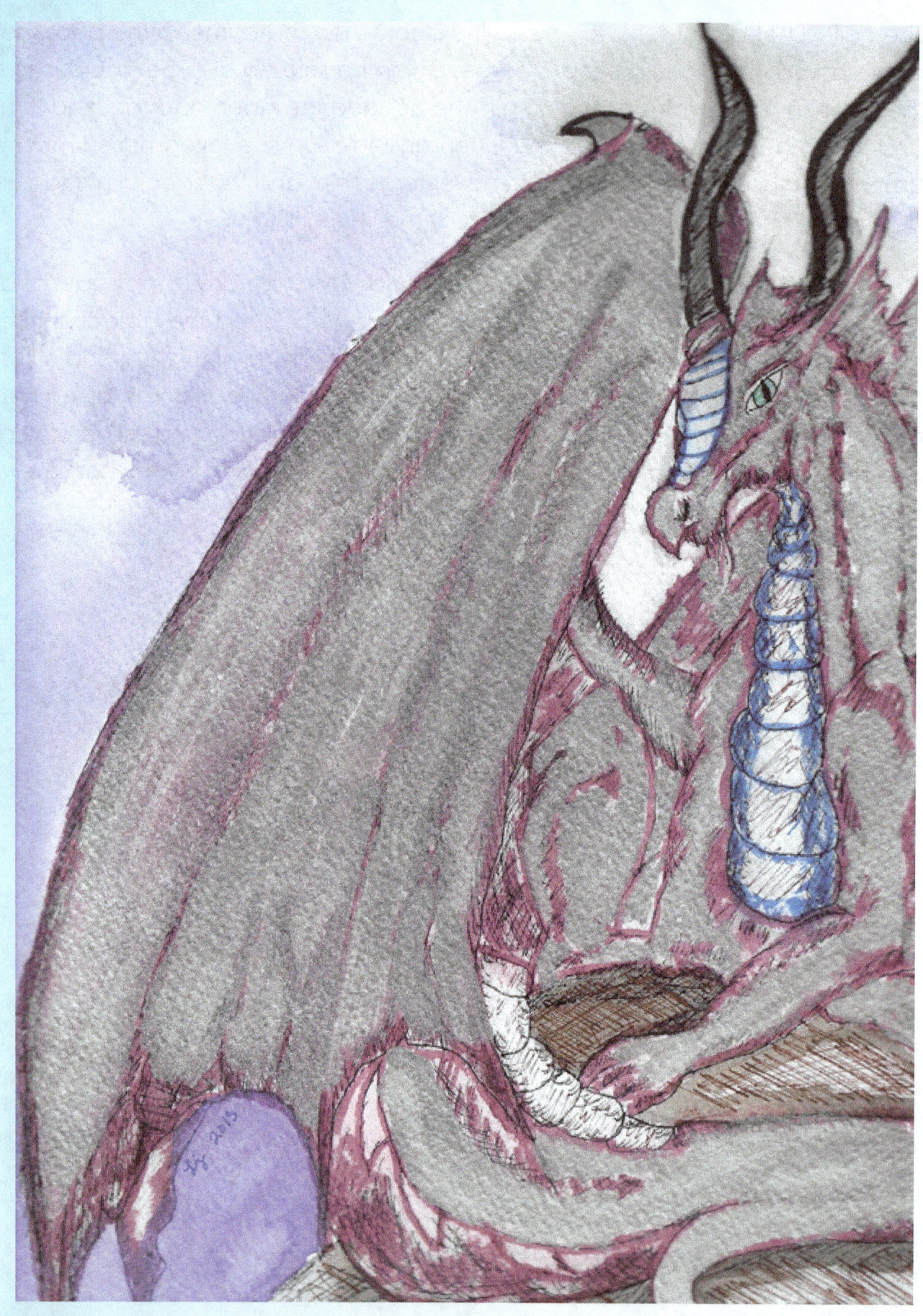

George made his way back to Amber and flew back to camp. They were greeted by Bella, Nermal and Rosa poor Midnight he looked so tired the dragonettes kept him very busy asking questions playing hide and seek and poor Midnight was so glad they were back and hugged Amber appreciating her skills caring for the dragonettes and being there for him and their family.

Soon it was time to move on they had a good time but it was time to fly and the babies were wanting to fly again so they packed up and set off just as the sun was rising setting off towards Ashlie's home enjoying the time, they spent flying together they skirted a storm and had to land until it passed and watched the lighting streak across the sky.

The babies were afraid at first by the loud noise and the lighting but with their parents and George by their sides they enjoyed the storm.

After it passed the air smelled so clean and fresh and the world was brighter on, they flew as they got closer to Ashlie's home, they used more caution there were many who hunted and would hunt them if they could.

George made his way to the castle and got Ashlie to come with him after they hugged each other Ashlie had missed her friends very much and had hoped they would visit as they made their way to their camp Ashlie remembered the dragonettes birthday party and the time spent with old friends.

Her family wanted to hear the stories over and over and excited to hear and listen to their mothers' stories amazed she had dragon friends and they remembered the birthday party and all the fun they had playing with the dragonettes. Ashlie was very happy they had come to visit her and her family and could not wait to see the dragonettes again.

As they made camp the dragonettes were chasing each other and rolling around in the dirt having fun. Ashlie had to laugh, it reminded her of her children playing. As soon as she saw them, she called them and they stopped what they were doing and almost tackled her with their greeting Amber and midnight reminded them that people are more fragile and to be gentle with Ashlie.

Ashlie hugged each of them and kissed each of them on the nose they had grown even bigger than the last time she saw them, they were so beautiful they had a glow about them and you could tell they were very loved.

Ashlie's twins were a handful. They were 8 years old. They loved to read and enjoyed playing music and playing in the tall spring grass. She would spend many hours brushing their long golden hair; they had blue eyes and fair skin. Many times there was grass and straw in their hair.

Their home was filled with love and understanding but there were rules as well manners were important as well as treating everyone with respect. Reading was encouraged and music and art were encouraged to follow their heart with their talents and strength. Their names were Anna and Jessica. They were brave and bold and got into many adventures that sometimes got them in trouble but with love and guidance they were very good children.

Ashlie hugged Midnight and he was happy to see her too. They worked out meeting the rest of the family and their household. They met at noon the next day planning a large picnic for all and met in the meadow that was in full bloom filled with wildflowers and butterflies everywhere.

When they had all assembled Ashlie introduced the dragons to them at first many were surprised, they thought she was just telling stories but they were there and soon everyone got to know them and interact with them without any fear or mistrust it was a pleasant day for all.

Activities were planned out for the week the dragonettes played with Anna and Jessica and it was fun to explore the area with their new friends but there was always a parent or George with them making sure they stayed safe.

They had lots of fun that week and made many new friendships but the time came to say goodbye. It was hard but promises were made to visit again. As they flew away, with good memories and feelings about the times spent with Ashlie's family.

The sun was setting as they flew on the glorious colors in the sky slowly turned dark and the stars came out brightly twinkling and shining making the dragonettes look with wonder at the world they were seeing with their parents and George.

The night was beautiful and the dragonettes had gotten stronger and were able to fly for long distances so they saw much more than when they were younger, they enjoyed the time spent flying at night and rested part of the mornings while their parents hunted and George would watch them.

Off to their favorite island they flew with the dragonettes in tow excited by all the sights, the ships and dolphins racing the wakes, shoals of silvery fish flashing in the sun as they swam close to the surface.

They were so excited and sometimes forgot themselves and would venture close to the ships and get too close to them but their parents and George quickly moved on protecting them and getting them safely away from harm.

They finally made it to the island! The young dragons played in the sand and chased the surf. Surprising quite a few crabs along the way and Rosa got pinched when her tail got too close to its hiding spot. It was hard not to laugh seeing a little crab clinging to her tail for dear life hoping it would not get eaten. The sun felt good and the water was warm so everyone decided to nap for a bit.

They awoke at 6pm and everybody was hungry so the meal was quickly prepared and everyone ate their fill rested and full they watched the sunset together knowing each day was a gift and to treasure every moment. They loved their children and George and in their heart their family was blessed by love and friendship that will always be special.

There were so many adventures they wanted to share with their children that they had to plan them out when the weather was right and there was time for them the dragonettes still had lots to learn and so they spent a week on the island.

They headed back to their village and all hands were needed to bring the harvest in. Winter was going to come soon and they needed to prepare, as they flew home, they thought about their adventures so far and how much their children had grown, a lot stronger and wiser for their travels.

But soon they needed to think about schooling and the harvest feast the village had after all the crops were harvested. They were glad to be home ready to get things set up and comfortable for the family again. The kids were bouncing around the cave happy to be home playing with each other.

Harvesting started and all worked together enjoying the weather and companionship the harvest brings many of the villagers set about cooking the feast breads, meats and vegetables and many wonderful desserts. The smells of wood smoke from the smoking meats filled the air, breads smelled wonderful and lots of roasting vegetables.

The dragonettes had so much fun digging up the potatoes and beets grabbing the yellow butternut squash and acorn squash sometimes eating them and being told not to eat them they listened but they really liked the vegetables.

Amber and Midnight hunted game for the feast and storage for the winter after all the harvest was in tables where set food was brought out music was played celebrating the bountiful harvests all the children played in the village as the adults set up the feasts up with the foods and other things. The villagers and dragons gathered and as they sat down for the feast everyone was grateful for the companionship of friends and being together.

After the feast there was a bonfire, the villagers danced and sang and the children played with the dragonettes enjoying the night as the harvest moon rose in the night sky laughing and playing into the night. Amber and Midnight collected their babies and made their way home with tired but happy kids tucking them in and kissing them goodnight.

Amber and Midnight fell asleep happy and healthy dreaming of their many travels together. Over the winter the family enjoyed a lovely winter holiday with George and his family. Christmas and New Years were spent in wonderful company and then took a long nap until spring as the sun warms the earth and the flowers were peeking from the earth.

They awoke to the songs of the returning birds and a warm spring rain.

The young dragons had grown a lot during their nap; they stretched and yawned and walked into the sunshine their parents joined them.

They all went to the waterfall and played in the water and searched for something to eat and then went to find George. They found George working on his parents' home painting the outside and his father was cutting wood. His mother was bringing out some lemonade and cookies for them when they spotted the dragon family coming. George was so happy to see them!

welcome spring

Big hugs and loving kisses were exchanged and the events that had occurred during their long nap were told to them it was a happy reunion for all. The young dragons had grown so much! Their parents were so proud of them they were gentle and loving, though there were challenges along the way together they worked and solved them. Compassion and patience, acceptance and strength as a family made them stronger and the most important thing was love. It is the strongest bond any family can have.

www.ingramcontent.com/pod-product-compliance
Lightning Source LLC
Chambersburg PA
CBHW081349070526
44578CB00005B/780